REVOLUTION II

SEVEN STEPS TO FREEDOM
WITHOUT BALLOTS & BULLETS

STEPHANIE AUGUSTE
Warrior Woman

Many Thanks...

To those who have supported my work in the liberty movement, I am especially grateful. As we know, this time in history has made it very challenging to speak out on issues concerning freedom. Doing so can cost us relationships, career opportunities, and more – but you have understood me and supported me. For this reason, I count you as a rare treasure, for which I am forever grateful.

Also, thanks to my oldest daughter, Brianna Auguste, for giving her artistic talents to doing the cover design for this book. What would I do without you, Brianna? Keep shining bright with your life. I love you and your sisters, Elise and Ambria.

And, most especially, I would like to thank my dear friend Ed Stein who leads the Wichita Falls Texas Tea Party. He has stood out in his support like no other and been an example to me of how we liberty-minded people should unify and support one another in our words and actions. Thank you, Ed. Your uncommon commitment to furthering the message of liberty in my life and the lives of others is something to which I aspire.

Most sincerely,

Stephanie Auguste
WARRIOR WOMAN

CONTENTS

SPECIAL NOTE: The e-book vorsion of this book is heavily hyperlinked with cited sources; however, those hyperlinks (indicated with highlighted text even in the print version) may also be accessed at www.warriorwoman212.com **under the book tab.**

In a nutshell...

A Mrs. Powel of Philadelphia asked Benjamin Franklin, "Well, Doctor, what have we got, a republic or a monarchy?" With no hesitation whatsoever, Franklin responded, "A republic, if you can keep it."

As this book approaches its release, the presidential election results for 2016 are also nearing their release. Usually, Americans are filled with hope during election time, but not this year. Many are worried – very worried – like never before. Some are saying that surely America could have produced better options than Hillary Rodham Clinton and Donald J. Trump – two people who have historically voted in favor of the Democratic Party, which has been the forerunner in furthering Progressivist (Socialist) policies that are arguably choking out freedom in the United States.

"But Trump has changed and will bring change," some argue. True enough, Trump has presented a platform that is remarkably more conservative than ever. Whether or not he will make good on delivering those promises has yet to be seen. We've learned all too well from the last eight years that promises are not enough to deliver a great job as a president or any politician.

1

Stephanie Auguste

As of this writing, both presidential candidates are not promising to cut government spending and over reach of the government. And even if they were, we have rampant evidence of voter fraud in this election, as we did in the 2012 election, and frankly many more.

This has led to many Americans feeling helpless and hopeless in terms of making a difference in this country, while others, like myself, have been led to ask what we can do to restore this republic that our Founding Fathers fought so hard to give.

How do we protect and restore freedom if our elections are rigged? Or, if the elections offer candidates who are seemingly lesser-of-two-evil choices? What do we do apart from warfare, as was done during the first American Revolution?

I ask these questions because something's got to give folks, or pretty soon this nation's sovereignty will be entirely lost for future generations.

In trying to find the answers to these questions, I've realized what has to give: We do! We have to change the way we live. Enough of this passivity and sense of powerlessness. Enough of this American way of thinking that we have to be quiet about politics because it only offends. Enough of believing that our interest and involvement in politics doesn't matter and is of no consequence. Enough! Time to take our power back! We live here and it's high-time we start acting like it!

Chances are that you agree with me, which is why you're reading this book – a book that is purposed to to show you how our everyday lifestyle choices either give our power away to the right causes or the wrong ones; either way, we do possess the power to force positive change, if only we will use that power wisely.

I began to understand this in 2012 after I saw so much voter fraud occur in the GOP against Ron Paul. And then, to my utter dismay, witnessed the mainstream media fall silent in covering this huge story of incredible injustice done to all Americans who vote. At first, I felt like "What's the use of trying?" as many Americans feel about politics, today. But slowly, I began learning from people like Fabian Calvo that we still have power, we just have to realize it and re-claim it, conscientiously. By the way, Fabian's video, How to Defeat the System, was the video that inspired me to write this book.

From that video and many other experiences since 2012, I came to understand that individually, we may not make a huge impact on freedom, but collectively we are a powerhouse. That's what I aim to show you in this book.

With some thoughtful changes to the way we live our daily lives, together we can protect and restore freedom in America, without ballots and without bullets.

Yes, it's possible! Please join me!

Stephanie Auguste

Let me share with you, in a nutshell, how you can:

1. Go Local
Bank and shop local to keep more dollars in your local economy.

2. Be a Job Creator
Instead of being a job taker, become a job creator - if not for others, then at least for yourself.

3. Live Naturally
Vote with your dollars to support non-GMO & organic food, alternative medicine, and natural practitioners.

4. Convert to Active Political Atheism
Choose principles of liberty over party-politics. Actively support real statesmen, and recall treasonous politicians across all party lines.

5. Support Alternative Media
Unplug from corporate media, and tune into alternative media. Actively support independent grassroots journalism, and add your voice to help fill this nation's void for real investigative journalism.

6. Starve the Beast
Stop paying for, and participating in, government programs which are against your moral and ethical conscience. Choose the brave path of civil disobedience.

7. Support the Right to Self-Defense
Vote, speak out, and demonstrate for American's rights to defend themselves. Support companies who arm American civilians.

Now, taking action on every step of this list is going to require considerable commitment, since it would require a revolutionary lifestyle change for most Americans. Of course, it requires nothing near the sacrifice of those who fought in the first Revolutionary War. Still, it's unlikely that most Americans can fulfill every action on this plan, because it isn't an easy one for all; however, when we do what we can, when we can, to the best of our ability, we will get closer to our goal of increased liberty.

Do you realize that much of our lost freedom was conquered by a quiet minority working relentlessly behind the scenes, through non-violent means? In the same way our liberties were lost, they can be found.

If just 3% of the population was responsible for winning the first American Revolution, then imagine the difference that just 3% of today's population can make by applying these non-violent solutions in America's second revolution.

Stay encouraged. Stay committed. Each of us can make a difference, for freedom's sake. ~ *Warrior Woman*

Stephanie Auguste

Bank And Buy Local

1

Small businesses are the backbone of our economy.

Ellen Tauscher

Bank and shop local to keep more dollars in your local economy.

Start banking and shopping more locally to keep more dollars in your local economy. And, while you're at it, use cash for purchases, as much as possible, because when you swipe a card, some of that money will likely leave your local economy, to cover global banking fees.

Leave the global banks (Bank of America, Chase, Citi, Wells Fargo) in preference of small locally-owned banks and credit unions. Most recently, we've seen headlines revealing that some of our largest banks were artificially propped up with $83 billion in taxpayer subsidies last year. Remember, just five years prior, in 2008, these same banks were bailed out with taxpayer dollars. Although, most people disagreed with that action, and even took to the streets nationwide in protest of this through the Occupy Wall Street movement in 2011, no meaningful change occurred. Clearly, effecting change at the global banking level requires more than electing politicians who promise change, while in reality hold banks as their greatest source of campaign contributions. It's going to take more than protesting en masse, as well.

What's the solution? Several years ago, the people at MoveYourMoneyProject.org released a compelling short video, encouraging viewers to move their money from the too big to fail global banking giants to small locally-owned banks and credit unions. They explained that when we do this, our dollars are reinvested back into local business and economic growth, rather than invested into global banking interests.

Leave the global retails chains (Wal-Mart, Target, Costco, Home Depot) in preference of small local stores, resale & consignment shops, and garage sales. Most recently, we've seen headlines telling us that companies like Wal-Mart are also being subsidized with taxpayer dollars. In one congressional report, it was revealed that for every $1 spent at Wal-Mart, Americans pay $3 to subsidize their employees with welfare benefits. At the same time, it seems nearly impossible to buy goods made in the USA today; most, as we well know, are made in China.

So, what can we do? Continue buying these products at full retail price, lining the pockets of globalist retailers outside our communities, while lamenting that we have no other choice? Absolutely not. We have more power than that. Let's take it back! Shop local stores and boutiques, featuring locally-made goods. Buy products at stores that feature the "Made Local" label. Shop resale, consignment, and garage sales – because although these will offer goods made outside of your area, any dollars spent on them will stay in your area. Expand your awareness of the local businesses available to you, and make it an exciting adventure getting find your next favorite place to shop. Expand your awareness of goods made in the USA, and support the companies that make them. Trying something new may be awkward at first, but once you get familiar with the great alternatives that surround you, you'll likely be happier that you did.

Beware of fake buy local campaigns. As the movement toward globalization increases, this counter movement toward localization has arisen to the challenge, with each side vying for their stake in our national economy. Interestingly, American Express has engaged in cause-related marketing to support local businesses, with their "shop small" campaign, occurring every black Friday, in recent years. Though their efforts appear commendable and noble on the surface, Americans should be aware that American Express is owned by the same man who has ownership of Wells Fargo, Costco, and other Fortune 500 Companies. So, using American Express, even when shopping local, will benefit global interests.

Another key item to consider is who is ultimately benefiting from a shop small campaign, if the target of spending is simply "small" businesses and the time frame only occurs one day out of the year? Small business, to some, may mean that little Starbucks coffee shop around the corner, when the real target needs to be the locally and privately owned coffee shop around the corner. Also, in order to be truly effective, we're obviously going to have to shop local more than one day a year. So, this cause-related marketing from American Express may be a step in the right direction, but it arguably does more for improving their image, than actually benefiting this cause.

Culturally, we've been conditioned to bank and shop global, and we've become comfortable with it. Granted, implementing the changes mentioned here won't be easy, but the pain of it is a far cry from what Americans sacrificed during the first American Revolution. For freedom's sake, make a decision today, if you will, to spend less of your money on the companies and interests that do not serve you and your local community.

To learn more and connect, visit Warrior Woman's Channel **and watch her playlist "**Bank And Buy Local**".**

Be A Job Creator

2

Entrepreneurship, entrepreneurship, entrepreneurship.
It drives everything: Job creation, poverty alleviation, innovation.

Elliott Bisnow

Instead of being a job taker, become a job creator;
if not for others, then at least for yourself.

Despite the glowing reports about how beautifully our economy has been rebounding from the recession of 2008, many readers know or know of someone who is collecting food stamps, social security for early retirement, or government-backed student loans for college.

Although we we're being told in 2013 through official reports that the current unemployment rate was 7%, those of us who were paying attention, knew that it was much, much worse. Some said that The real unemployment rate was more like 23% at that time, if one calculates these numbers to account for the non-working and under-employed, as was done during the depression. And, as if cooked books weren't enough, Americans were also experiencing the highest levels of inflation – a devalued dollar, with significantly crippled buying power – ever. Many gave up looking for work, but those who continued, often found opportunities with reduced pay and reduced hours of 30 or less, so companies could avoid paying the debilitating costs of Obamacare for their employees.

That was in 2013, but it is now 2016. Has the job market improved by now? What I can say as a job-hunter is that the opportunities have definitely increased, but the quality of these opportunities arguably has not. And, if you look at statistical reports coming from the Bureau of Labor & Statistics (BLS), this appears to be a documentated fact.

So, what's an average American job-seeker to do? Conventional wisdom says to improve your education in order to improve job opportunities; unfortunately, many graduates today have found that what awaits them after graduation is not a job, but student loan debt that they cannot repay. And, many speculate that a student loan bubble is on the brink of bursting, much like the housing bubble of '08, as more graduates default on their loans because of an anemic job market. The good news about this bad news is that this economic situation has left many with plenty of free time on their hands, along with a good measure of angst, to passionately delve into understanding the true source of these economic troubles in hopes of finding real solutions.

Return to creating goods – a tried and true path to prosperity. A solid search on the internet reveals that America's economic rise and fall has much to do with whether or not we are creating goods – not services. When our manufacturing started going overseas in the 1970s we began the slow downward spiral of visibly loosing our economic strength. And, if you look at the ghost towns of China today you see a living testament to all that America's middle-class has lost in this transfer of wealth. In China, their growth in manufacturing (that came from America) has prospered their middle-class so abundantly, that they have invested in real estate; problem is, no one is buying it, so all the pristine and expansive development sits vacant. To see these Chinese ghost towns is truly astonishing, as it gives material evidence of how far-reaching the economic loss of our manufacturing has been to America.

Fight back! Take back your creative power to be prosperous! Granted, this is easier said than done. Regulations against small businesses in America are worse than ever. And, accounts of fraud at the Small Business Administration (SBA) have surfaced. This organization, which is supposedly purposed to help small businesses with loans and the acquisition of government contracts, has been caught giving $1 trillion dollars over the last decade to Fortune 500 companies, with very little media coverage and no legal justice.

In the midst of this uphill economic battle, small business owners of today are less prepared than ever to think and lead effectively as independent creators. As it turns out, we have U.S. Department of Education experts like Charlotte Iserbyt and John Tayor Gatto warning us that since the turn of the 18th century, corporate philanthropy groups, like the Rockefeller Foundation, have invested in and influenced the coursework of public education for Americans to purposefully indoctrinate students to become employees – not creators, leaders, and inventors. So, as Americans become increasingly unable to compete in this degree-saturated job market - where the number of unemployed is three times that of the number of jobs available - they are feeling unbelievable pressure to become self-reliant, with the limited economic support and leadership skills necessary to be a success.

How can your skill set enrich your local economy, given the current adversity? This is a question more Americans are asking themselves, as the economy forces them to make a financial way – when there seems to be no way - to pay their bills. By surrounding themselves with other small local business owners, becoming well-connected and well-mentored, they are over-coming the odds. They are overcoming mental blocks to creativity, years of financial illiteracy, and deficits in leadership skills.

With crony-capitalism arguably in its final death throes, extreme measures have been taken to curb growth in the free market through burdensome rules and regulations, which are imposed in the name of the public safety. Still, the free market is fighting a good fight. For example, a group of anarchists in Detroit have occupied abandoned neighborhoods, set up community garden co-ops, and started providing community services that the bankrupted city government can no longer provide. In Houston, a group called Conscious Resistance Network has initiated Freedom Cell Networks to teach people how to peacefully and creatively assert their sovereignty, regardless of which locale they live. Inspiring stories like this, show us how alive this country's spirit is to thrive, and how we can greatly impact the bleakest regions with meaningful change, against all odds.

What will you do in this time of great adversity? Will you be job taker? Or, a job creator? Sooner or later, you're probably going to have to ask yourself this question. Sooner or later, the government will run out of money to subsidize Americans with food stamps, social security, unemployment benefits, and student loans. It simply cannot support these expenditures without end, with as many un- and under-employed Americans as we have, currently.

It's simple math folks! When the government is no longer able to artificially prop-up our economy, and give cooked-book reports about the condition of our workforce, then the illusion of prosperity and the false optimism will end. For freedom's sake, let's be prepared to let this end of illusions be the beginning of restoring this nation's wealth to its rightful owners.

To learn more and connect, visit Warrior Woman's Channel **and watch her playlist "**Be A Job Creator**".**

Also, visit Meetup.com to find groups of other independent professionals, entrepreneurs, and business owners in your area. And, visit Lynda.com to acquire affordable and quick professional skill development. And finally, visit the National Business Incubation Association (NBIA) to find the business incubator nearest to you.

Stephanie Auguste

Live Naturally

Let food be thy medicine and medicine be thy food.

Hippocrates

Vote with your dollars to support non-GMO & organic food, alternative medicine, and natural practitioners.

Is it just me, or have you noticed that people are struggling with sickness and disease, more than ever? Have you noticed cancer and infertility treatment centers have sprouted up around the country, like never before? No, I don't think it's just me who has noticed this trend. According to a recent article, 70% of Americans take prescription drugs. And, despite our claims of having the best medical system in the world, we have the worst maternal death rates of any industrialized country, we suffer higher rates of disease, and we live shortened lifespans when compared to other wealthy countries.

What's the solution? Well, our government seems to think the solution is more government, in the form of socialized healthcare, but I beg to differ.

Stephanie Auguste

The solution is in the rejection of the current medical tyranny overtaking our culture; however, to be successful in this overthrow, we must move beyond the philosophical and into the practical. What does this mean? This means that we have to vote with our dollars daily to support alternative and natural health care practitioners, instead of conventional ones – from birth to death – unless, of course, an emergency or crisis-situation demands otherwise. And, this means that we have to vote with our dollars daily to find safe and natural remedies that prevent and treat the root cause of our health problems, instead of expensive and dangerous big-pharma 'solutions' that merely mask symptoms, while creating more symptoms for us to mask. Also, this means that we have to vote with our dollars daily to support the local growers and suppliers of non-GMO and organic food, instead of those global big-agri companies that are supplying us with polluted franken-foods at popular fast food chains and at our grocery stores.

Yes, I know this isn't going to be easy. In fact, sometimes, we're probably going to fall off the wagon, so to speak, in meeting this goal because it is so ingrained in us to pop pills in our mouths, nuke food in our microwaves, and eat cheap food in our cars. However, though we may fail at times in making this lifestyle change, living a more health-conscious lifestyle bit-by-bit will positively impact us not only on an individual level, but also on a collective level in the market place, as retailers realize they must get rid of their garbage or get taken out with it.

At risk of sounding bossy, I will – for brevity's sake – outline some **actions and resources** you can take to make this philosophy a practical way of life:

18

• **For Babies:** Give birth to your babies at home with midwives, unless you have a high-risk pregnancy. Breastfeed for at least the first 6 months, and use all-natural goat's milk as an alternative to formula. Avoid infant formula. Avoid so-called 'nursery' bottled water that is fortified with fluoride. Avoid infant circumcision. Learn how to boost your immune system naturally, instead of using vaccines and antibiotics.

• **For Children:** Hire a naturopath, instead of a pediatrician, for your children's healthcare. Use biological or holistic dentistry, instead of conventional dentistry – to avoid toxic fillings and fluoridated toothpaste. Establish healthy eating and hygiene habits during the formative years, ages 1-7. Use natural soaps, instead of commercialized petroleum-based detergent soaps. Have pets because they help children to naturally build up immunities.

• **For Adults:** Continue to refuse vaccines, such as flu shots. Continue to support natural practitioners, such as naturopaths, chiropractors, and holistic dentists. Start a garden. Support your local farmer's market, or at least buy from the organic and natural sections in your grocery store. Buy products labeled Non-GMO Project. Support eateries like Chipotle who have decided to go GMO-free or Chick-Fil-A who have decided to go antibiotic-free. Or, better yet, find the small local eateries that are already all-natural in your community and support them. Learn how to use herbs, essential oils, and other natural ingredients to cope with common ailments and make healthy alternatives to household products.

Granted, these recommendations are very unconventional. In fact, it is likely that you read some of them and thought they were crazy, because we have all been conditioned to think this way by those who profit from such mindsets. So, before you dismiss anything here as 'crazy talk', please take another look at what you've learned to trust. Consider that you may have not been given all the information. Do some investigation on the truth about America's health crisis, for yourself.

For our health's sake, for our freedom's sake, let's overthrow this country's debilitating medical tyranny daily, one dollar at a time!

To learn more and connect, visit Warrior Woman's Channel **and watch her playlist, "**Live Naturally**".**

Also, visit Mercola.com to learn the latest findings on your health conditions, from a trusted doctor.

And, visit NatrualNews.com to learn the latest health-related news, from a trusted source.

Convert to Active Political Atheism

4

*I am a political atheist... Politics has become a religion
and I don't bown down to political gods.*
Gerald Celente

C hoose principles of liberty over party-politics.
Actively support real statesmen, and recall
treasonous politicians across all party lines.

"Vote them out", I often hear it said when people are
dissatisfied with politicians. Sounds easy enough, but what
does that mean? Often, in America, it means voting for the
politician hated the least, through a process that has
repeatedly proven itself to be unethical. Although a reported
58% of Americans claim that both Republicans and
Democrats are doing a poor job, and that a third party is
needed, they continue to vote against the person they hate
the most, rather than build up the candidates who need to be
elected. Even when voters study candidates closely, and
support the true statesmen, they then have to deal with voter
fraud, from local to national levels.

Stephanie Auguste

In 2012, far too many Americans didn't know about voter fraud like they do in this election year. Even so, when the subject is mentioned, far too many still don't know about it, because these incidents are conveniently ignored by corporate mainstream media. Or, it's openly denied and downplayed. And why is this? As some of us know, the media is often in bed with the very politicians they're highlighting in their programming. We're seeing this with Hillary Clinton in 2016, with recent Wikileaks of emails showing that they American media is acting as a virtual public relations firm for Clinton. But really, this is nothing new. This was going on during the 2012 election, if not prior.

For those who need to get up to speed on what happened then, here's a primer of clickable links:

- GOP primary level and RNC convention
- DNC Chicago voters
- Rigged voting machines
- Debate commission rigged

As if the stinking thinking from parties wasn't enough, we also have some stinking thinking from voters, who've been trained to mindlessly vote straight ticket and be manipulated through rhetoric to support policies that they would not ordinarily support. This allegiance to parties over principles has gotten us into a great deal of trouble, and will continue to do so, if we don't break out of tribal mentalities that motivate us to dichotomize everything - as if everything is as simple as choosing between things like Chevy vs. Ford, Coke vs. Pepsi, and so on. If we continue applying this thinking of Republican vs. Democrat, then we will continue to be manipulated by tyrants in both parties against our own interests in liberty that should unite us all. If there is any dichotomy that we should fix our minds upon, let it be about tyranny vs. liberty.

There is no left or right. There is only liberty or tyranny.

Don't believe me? Remember this: the next time a candidate simply parrots a popular phrase among his or her constituents like, "secure the borders" or "women's reproductive health rights" and magically gets an automatic round of applause at debates – that is no accident. The GOP, for example, has hired Frank Luntz to study Americans to find which words or phrases can be used to manipulate voters into supporting whatever the GOP desires of them to support. What's to stop the DNC from doing the same? Nothing. Absolutely, nothing. And, who's to say that they haven't? We now have video records of them admitting that they've hire mentally unstable people to disrupt the meetings of political opponents and bused in voters to artificially inflate polls for over 50 years.

So, what happens when someone like Ron Paul – that is liberty-minded – tries to enter politics and change the conversation to a more honest, non-manipulative one? Well, I've followed one such candidate in the last four years named Derrick Grayson. Based on his reports of his experience, the media has failed to mention him as even running for office and participating in debates. And, the GOP leadership is backing who Grayson refers to as their 'royals'; these are the candidates who continue talking like conservatives while voting as if they are not. Though Grayson has done incredibly parties to our current two-party system, would undermine the objective of keeping us divided and distracted. It would reveal the false, scripted, pseudo-war between the Democrats and Republicans.

Stephanie Auguste

Don't believe me? Well consider this: every President we've seen in our lifetimes has steadily moved us in the same direction of less liberty and more tyranny. Yes, Republicans like to remember the Bush family with fondness, however the Bush family has questionable connections that do not serve We The People, and George Jr.'s policies, such as the Patriot Act (which should have been more accurately named the UnPatriot Act or the Violate your 4th Amendment Act) paved the way for Obama's NDAA, NSA-wiretapping, FEMA camps, and more. Think about it: as far back as our beloved President Reagan, we heard about how he was going to 'secure the border'. That was almost 40 years ago! Has it happened? How many politicians – Republican or Democrat – have you heard promising to 'secure the borders'? Has it ever happened? Will it ever…?

At this very moment, we have both Republicans and Democrats doing more to 'secure' the Ukrainian border than we have ever seen them do for our own.

Think about it.

Not too long ago, both parties were trying to push an Immigration Reform Bill through, which should more accurately be named, "Amnesty for Illegal Cheap Labor Bill" or "Trojan Horse for Biometrics Bill".

Think about it: who does this benefit?

After 40 years of promising to secure the borders, we've come to this. Do you really think this is an accident? Or, that it can be blamed on just one party? If we ignore the rhetoric, if we become blind to the party brands, and we pay attention to the results they give – it becomes obvious that they are working lockstep with one another to achieve the same outcome – less liberty, more tyranny.

Our founding fathers warned us that this would happen with a two-party system:

> *There is nothing which I dread so much*
> *as a division of the republic into two great parties,*
> *each arranged under its leader, and concerting measures*
> *in opposition to each other.*
> *This, in my humble apprehension, is to be dreaded*
> *as the greatest political evil under our Constitution.*
> **John Adams**

So, what are we going to do about it? Keep voting as usual? I say no. If you feel led to vote, then do so, but don't be passive about it. Keep these parties and voting booths accountable, like the Ron Paul voters did at the primary level in 2012. Support grassroots liberty-minded candidates with money, and by spreading their message on your social media. And, in the mean time, practice the lifestyle that brings us greater liberty by going local, being a job creator, living naturally, converting to political atheism, and more.

As a registered Republican, who swallowed the truth pill during the 2012 elections, I can tell you it hasn't been an easy one to swallow, but the sooner we take our 'medicine' the better. The sooner we get healthy, and free from the religion of party politics, the better. So, please join me in becoming an active political atheist, so we can get our liberty back, regardless of parties and their corruption.

To learn more and connect, visit Warrior Woman's Channel **and watch her playlist,** "Convert to Active Political Atheism".

Support Alternative Media

5

If you can control the information, you can control people.

Tom Clancy

Unplug from corporate media, and tune into alternative media. Actively support independent grassroots journalism, and add your voice to help fill this nation's void for real investigative journalism.

Surprise! Surprise! The latest headlines show that censoring and propaganda reign supreme at CBS, CNN, NBC, and RT, according to their news anchors. But, really, is it that hard to believe? Reports came out several years ago demonstrating that most of the world's media is scripted, faked, and owned by a mere 6 companies. And, the profession of investigative journalism in America is nearly non-existent.

With that kind of control on information dissemination, can any one honestly trust that the news they're getting is fair and unbiased, no matter who's claiming to deliver it? I say no.

Stephanie Auguste

The control of information is something the elite always does, particularly in a despotic form of government. Information, knowledge, is power. If you can control information, you can control people.
Tom Clancy

Worsening the controls that exist on our mainstream, corporate-owned media, are the detrimental effects of continual viewing. Some scientists claim that the electronic waves that TVs emit cause viewers' minds to go into a trance-like state, an alpha-state to be exact, where they become passive viewers, rather than active participants in a dialogue that engages critical thinking. Additionally, TV 'programming' is has been argued by some to be just that – programming or brainwashing, used for the purpose of manipulating the masses. It's been said that soap operas and dramas were created for women to artificially live out their passions, while sports were created for men to artificially live out their tribal tendencies, without either gender actually doing so. The end result is that we collectively become disengaged with our own individual destinies. Instead, we align ourselves with mental uploads from our TVs, much like computers that are programmed, to identify with a cultural identity elicited by fictional emotional story lines from our entertainment, rather than logical reasoning. Some claim, that this is why many people today cannot think or reason for themselves. Instead, they cling to political correctness, and they care not for facts but for having others accept and agree with them.

Shortly, the public will be unable to reason or think for themselves. They'll only be able to parrot the information they've been given on the previous night's news.
Zbigniew Brzezinski

The good news is that all this can be overcome when we understand the conditioning and control that advertising, public relations, propaganda can have on us – collectively and individually. For those who are having a hard time believing that psychological warfare can be used against societies, consider that the Soviet Union had a Ministry of Culture staffed by 'cultural leaders' for this purpose. If one country can do this, then what makes you think it can't happen elsewhere? Consider that it probably already has happened in a place called Hollywood. Consider, for example, how in the last 5 years we have seen a massive increase in TV programming that promotes the Lesbian, Gay, Bisexual, and Transgeneder (LGBT) lifestyle. Now, how does a segment of our society that represents roughly 3% of our population suddenly leverage this much disproportionate airtime on TV, if not for it fulfilling some greater agenda by those controlling the purse strings of mass media outlets? What agenda might the LGBT movement be fulfilling? Consider that goal #26 of the "Communist Manifesto", written in 1963 called for encouraging same sex relations to break down American culture, and make way for communism. Now, you may connect whatever dots you like, and draw whatever conclusions you like, but consider that not everything that happens is random, especially in business. And, when we see various media outlets seemingly working in harmony to disseminate similar messages, as if orchestrated, there may actually be some planning behind this, based on a unifying agenda.

It's easier to fool people
than to convince them that they have been fooled.
Mark Twain

Stephanie Auguste

Fortunately, we have some independent grassroots citizen journalists who have risen to challenge these agendas with agendas of their own, and they're gaining momentum. Mass media has had record low ratings in recent years, which continue to falter. In this time of information warfare, independents like Alex Jones have been demonized and characterized as 'crazy' and 'extreme' for challenging official positions and narratives. While this kind of rhetoric may work on the weak-minded, it has only propelled others to inquire further. And those who inquire further, as I did, often check out Jones' sources, only to find that he's not making this stuff up; he's actually re-reporting official news and research from others that has oftentimes been buried by other news. Consequently, independent and investigative journalists like Alex Jones continue to see their audience increase, while mainstream media's drops. The political establishment has tried to push back their influence by proposing legislation, like

SOPA and PIPA, that would control information on the internet, which has made the democratization of press possible. Additionally, politicians, like California's Dianne Feinstein have tried to introduce legislation that would define who is considered a journalist and protected from prosecution. This move - which is reminiscent of George Orwell's 'Ministry of Truth' in his classic book "1984" - was not successful for now. Unfortunately, despite this victory for First Amendment lovers, we must keep an eye on politicians continually re-packaging, re-naming, and re-introducing legislation that controls information, among other things.

First they ignore you, then they ridicule you,
then they fight you, and then you win.
Mahatma Gandhi

Now, I've done all I can up to this point to make a strong case (full of cited sources) for readers to unplug from corporate media, and tune into alternative media, if they haven't already. This is not to say that you should completely shut out mainstream media sources, but rather to compare their reports to that of others online.

"You can't believe everything online", I've heard a lot of baby-boomers say, who've been trained for decades to trust the TV. To them I say, "You obviously can't trust everything on TV either, yet you keep watching it? Tsk. Tsk."

The days of trusting others to think and make things right for us are over. Let's learn our lesson about where the path of passivity leads. Let's tread a new path by supporting independent journalists such as:

Ben Swann
Breitbart
David Seaman

Derrick Grayson
Drudge Report
Fabian4Liberty
Mark Dice
Mat Larson
Next News Network
PJ Media
We Are Change

We can show our support through viewership, money bombs, and sharing their content on our social media. And, while we're at it, we can affect our sphere of influence by creating original content – through blogs, YouTube videos, and more – that will further awaken others to truth, for freedom's sake!

Stephanie Auguste

To learn more and connect, visit Warrior Woman's Channel **and watch her playlist, "**Support Alternative Media**".**

6

Starve The Beast

Disobedience is the true foundation of liberty.
The obedient must be slaves.
Henry David Thoreau

top paying for, and participating in, government programs which are against your moral and ethical conscience. Choose the brave path of civil disobedience.

Let's face it: We're up against a Goliath. Worse, we're up against a Goliath that's being fed by the fruits of our own labor. So, just as simply as it was once proposed that we shut down the NSA-spying facility in Utah by turning off its water supply, I say we can and should shut down government corruption by turning off its monetary supply. How else will we get them to stop financing terrorists like Al-Qaeda? How else will we get them to stop awarding grants to the nation's largest abortion provider, Planned Parenthood? How else will we get them to stop pushing Common Core curriculum and other forms of state-sponsored indoctrination programs on our children?

As radical as it may sound to say stop paying taxes and stop subjecting your children to the school system, consider how the alternatives have worked out for us. We've heard outcries from parents against Common Core, yet few schools have

33

recanted their efforts to embrace this program. We've seen constituents outraged over taxpayer-subsidized infanticide, illegal immigration, terrorism, endless unconstitutional wars, and more; yet, no matter how people vote, no matter how many petitions they sign, no matter how much they complain to Congress, it continues. So, what viable options remain, except to simply slay the beast by starving it of funds to thrive?

I realize that many will object to this simply because of their Christian faith that teaches obedience to those in authority, but may I remind you that you and I (that is, We The People) are the authority in this nation. This is not a monarchy; it is supposed to be a Republic. Unfortunately, we've been conditioned to see our public servants and representatives as our authorities. Worse, our church leaders have used twisted teachings of Romans 13 to reinforce this false belief, just as was done in the days of Hitler. Some wonder how moral Germans sat idle as Jews were being openly persecuted and killed; the answer is Romans 13, a passage of scripture that's said to been a favorite of Hitler's and propagandists of his time. Today, we see the same thing happening as innocent children are murdered through abortion, and moral Americans sit idle and complicit by paying taxes to fund it. Even when confronted with this, Christians often defend their actions with twisted teachings of Romans 13 and yet another false doctrine pervading the church: the pre-tribulation doctrine. You see, by believing that God is going to rescue (or rapture them) before these evil days get too bad, they absolve themselves of any responsibility to fight the good fight of faith, and they believe the lie that they will escape the consequences of refusing to occupy this nation with bold and brave righteousness until He returns.

The reason why church leaders are teaching these false doctrines is two-fold: 1) they have been taught these doctrines in seminary schools that are often financed by the New World Order crowd, and 2) they are incentivized with 5013c tax-exempt status' to remain silent on political matters. Consequently, the typical sheep's interest in politics is not far from that of their typical shepherds: silence and complicity.

> *The only thing necessary for the triumph of evil*
> *is for good men to do nothing.*
> **Edmund Burke**

Now, consider that people are not only being taught silence and complicity at church, but also at public schools and institutions of higher education. Currently, Common Core curriculum has been scorned as socialist propaganda with the intention of deliberately dumbing-down and frustrating the next generation. Is this curriculum really the first of its kind in America? Or, have they beefed up their methods, and we're just now noticing?

Whistleblowers who worked within or under the US Department of Education, Charlotte Iserbyt and John Gatto, explain that the answer is the latter. Common Core is nothing new, it's just the same state indoctrination program that schools have been using, only this time it's on steroids with more of a socialist bend. Generations prior were subjected to teachings that also perpetuated a 'collective' mentality, for the purpose of creating good workers in the corporate hive. Who started all of this? Who financed this? The same financially-elite families that financed our nation's top seminary schools. You see, they didn't want people being trained to become innovators, creators, and independent business owners; basically, they didn't want competitors. They wanted you, your

children, and grandchildren, to become good little assets to their company - a cog in their corporate machine, if you will. And now, with Common Core, they want you and yours to become good little assets for the corporatist-government hive.

I don't want a nation of thinkers. I want a nation of workers.
John D Rockefeller

*They want people just smart enough to operate
the machines and do the paperwork,
and just dumb enough to passively accep
the shittier working conditions,
reduced pay, and reduced benefits.*
George Carlin

With those quotes in mind, does it now make sense why subjects like rhetoric, that teach critical thinking and the art of persuasion, were removed from our schools' curriculum? Consider what one must intellectually and financially overcome in this country in order to think critically. Consider the fate of conservatives who thought critically of this government, and how the very system they've funded – namely the IRS – was used against them for the purpose of political oppression. And, this is the same government organization getting armed to the teeth – paid for, again, with our tax dollars – supposedly for the enforcement of the Obamacare health mandate. Now, ask yourselves, do you want to pay for this? Do you want to continue to pay for your own oppression and that of others? I'm guessing your answer is like mine: Hell NO!

So, consider my solution: Stop paying for, and participating in, government programs which are against your moral and ethical conscience.

For freedom's sake, choose the brave path of civil disobedience.

Starve the beast!

To learn more and connect, visit Warrior Woman's Channel **and watch her playlist, "**Starve The Beast**".**

Stephanie Auguste

Support The Right To Self-Defense

7

No freeman shall ever be debarred the use of arms.

Thomas Jefferson

I've lost track of all the reports I've heard of mass shootings in America. We've heard of the Colorado theatre shooting, the Sandy Hook school shooting, and the Fort Hood's military base shooting. I could go on... More importantly, however, can we consider what's common to all these events that the media is *not* discussing? They all involve shooters who were on psychotropic drugs and they all occurred in gun free zones. Instead of investigating the role that these factors play in mass shooting events, the media has consistently used these stories to persuade Americans to ban weapons, call for greater limitations on weapons, and urge registration. In some cases, such as one in Connecticut, residents were forced to turn in their weapons or face imprisonment. After it was apparent that the vast majority of gun owners in Connecticut did not and would not turn in their guns, reports surfaced that a slow-confiscation was underway in the state, which involved profiling motorists for traffic stops, which in-turn resulted in car searches, which in-turn led to confiscation and jail. Bottom line: Americans are having their guns confiscated bit-by-bit, behind a false rationale that it will make America safe from mass shooting tragedies.

Stephanie Auguste

Why do we keep seeing these mass shootings? It's for the same reason that we'll continue to see them, and why the media conveniently chooses not to highlight the good news stories that show how law-abiding concealed carry Americans have protected victims from armed criminals. At the root of all cherry-picking of news stories is the fact that the United Nations (UN) is pushing for global gun confiscation through the UN Arms Treaty, and in March 2014, President Obama has signed a statement reaffirming his commitment to civilian disarmament.

As this plan for global disarmament continues, we'll also continue to see the "gun control is for your safety" narrative persist in our media and in our public schools. Even though the residents of Chicago have recently enjoyed the benefits of implementing concealed-carry laws, which arguably resulted in the lowest gun crime rates since 1958, the media and left-leaning police chief of Chicago refuse to acknowledge the law's impact. Instead, they credit their law enforcement talent, getting guns off the street, and they continue to caution people against owning guns for their own protection. Their line of reasoning is much like that of Colorado democrat, Joe Salazar, who thinks that women should just urinate or vomit to avoid being raped, rather than defend themselves with a gun. This kind of rhetoric is not only reaching adults through TV, but also children through public schooling.

Through common core curriculum, children are being indoctrinated to misunderstand the purpose of the Founding Father's establishment of the Second Amendment. Textbooks depict the right to bear arms as being for militias-only, and specific for combating the British. Furthermore, they fail to

40

mention that throughout history, tyrannical governments, which engaged in democide (mass murder by government), confiscated guns and made them illegal. Historically, gun registration precedes confiscation; in fact, we have Feinstein, Holder, and other politicians on record that they want to confiscate our guns, and that our children should be 'brainwashed' daily in school to support this.

Ironically, Holder and other pro gun control politicians have been accused of gun-running in Mexico, which has resulted in the deaths of many Mexicans and border patrol agents. While Americans are being told to disarm, Mexico's drug cartels are being armed by our government, and our government is also arming itself to the teeth.

DHS is on record for stockpiling 1.6 billion hollow-point bullets, that are explicitly for the purpose of killing – not target practice. They've also purchased 7000 auto assault rifles, along with the IRS. And, we've seen in influx of police departments getting equipped with armored vehicles and urban combat gear. Just who are they preparing to fight, and why? Perhaps DHS' $2 million purchase of target practice posters entitled, "No More Hesitation", which depict the

elderly, children, and pregnant women in residential locations lend us a clue. And, if that isn't enough, consider that one SWAT team cop has written extensively about how cops are being conditioned to see their fellow Americans as their enemies and the neighborhoods they serve as battlefields akin to those in Afghanistan.

What's happening here folks, is that we are being propagandized to give up our right to self-defense. We're

Stephanie Auguste

getting this propaganda in our media, our children are getting it in public schools. We're being policed by and for a citizenry that largely doesn't understand their rights and why they should be defending them. And, it's all by design to have the entire globe disarmed by the UN, and rendered defenseless against any of their tyrannical one world order plans.

Those of you who have read this far and still have the naïve thought that gun confiscation can never happen in America need to understand that it already has. Remember Katrina? Guns were brutally confiscated there in the name of public safety. The result: women were raped repeatedly, homes were robbed, and Americans were mugged without any defense. Even in non-catastrophic natural disaster events, like the Fort Hood shooting, we see that it takes 15 minutes for the police to respond, leaving unarmed Americans – even ex-military men, mind you – completely defenseless. Yet, these people keep pushing for gun control, arguing that only the police should have guns for your safety.

The truth is, gun control makes criminals and out-of-control governments safer – NOT you. So, actively resist this plan for disarmament, even if you don't own firearms. Warn your friends and family. For freedoms sake, let's make sure that if this nation goes down, it doesn't go down without a good, honest Founding-Father-style fight.

To learn more and connect, visit Warrior Woman's Channel **and watch her playlist, "**Support the Right to Self-Defense**".**

ABOUT THE AUTHOR

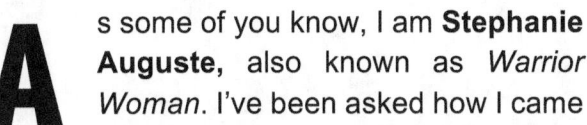

Warrior Woman

As some of you know, I am **Stephanie Auguste,** also known as *Warrior Woman*. I've been asked how I came up with the name *Warrior Woman* and the answer is that I am a fighter - especially, when it comes to matters of freedom. And, I can get pretty passionate about it! That might be partly because I've got it in my blood, as the descendant of warriors on my father's side of the family. We've had men fighting for freedom in America since the Revolutionary War. So, you see, it more or less comes naturally for me to want to fight for freedom, even as a woman armed with a pen, keyboard, or microphone.

For me, *freedom* goes beyond politics - it's a way of life. *It's a lifestyle!* For this reason, I'll occasionally speak on topics such as alternative health, spirituality, and homeschooling. As a matter of fact, vaccine choice is one of my hot button topics. As a mother of three completely vaccine-free children - who, by the way, has no regrets - I've been asked to publicly speak about this and I've worked with a grassroots groups to protect vaccine choice in Texas, among other things.

As I continue to learn along with you more about issues concerning freedom, it's occurred to me that we're awakening ourselves and others to a life lived with more freedom. That's a life we were destined and purposed to have. So, thanks for keeping in touch with me at warriorwoman212.com and sharing my information with others. Together, let's drop truth bombs for freedom's sake! ~ *Warrior Woman*

www.ingramcontent.com/pod-product-compliance
Lightning Source LLC
Chambersburg PA
CBHW070231290526
45789CB00004B/1571